HENRI DE TOULOUSE-LAUTREC

T&J

Published by TAJ Books International LLP 2012
27 Ferndown Gardens
Cobham
Surrey
KT11 2BH
UK
www.tajbooks.com

All notations of errors or omissions (author inquiries, permissions) concerning
the content of this book should be addressed to
info@tajbooks.com.

ISBN 978-1-84406-197-6

Printed in China.
1 2 3 4 5 16 15 14 13 12

HENRI DE TOULOUSE-LAUTREC

T&J

BY SANDRA FORTY

HENRI DE TOULOUSE-LAUTREC

November 24, 1864–September 9, 1901

Henri de Toulouse-Lautrec was one of the great personalities of *fin de siècle* Paris, a famous and popular figure known by, and knowing, everyone who mattered in bohemian circles. He was a true aristocrat descended from ancient lineages and could mingle in the highest echelons of society, but his preferred company was that of the entertainers and the shady inhabitants of Parisian nightlife around the notorious and dangerous district of Montmartre. Toulouse-Lautrec is usually classified as a post-impressionist painter, along with his contemporaries Gauguin and van Gogh. In common with many artists, Toulouse-Lautrec had to struggle to gain acceptance, but unlike his peers, his fight was not so much for his art as for himself. Because of his short stature (5 feet 1 inch), he faced prejudice and derision. To assuage the hurt, he took to drink, and ultimately that as much as anything hastened his early death. He was a multi-talented artist who became famous for recording all the excitement and color of late-nineteenth-century Paris, especially the more exuberant, sexually expressive side of the city, namely, the nightclubs, cafés, restaurants, dance halls, and brothels.

In his spiritual home of Paris, Lautrec gravitated toward the marginalized masses who lived on the edge of society and for whom he felt great empathy and sympathy. He was fascinated by the seedy and dissolute side of the city, an entire slice of life completely ignored by polite society, yet just as relevant as any other existence. For many people, the world he exposed was shocking and beyond their comprehension; most citizens had nothing—openly—to do with such low life.

Lautrec could have had an easy life as a society portrait painter, but he preferred to paint the ordinary people of Montmartre, especially the streetwalkers and entertainers, many of whom were also his friends. Among the social outcasts of Parisian nightlife, Lautrec was very comfortable and openly welcomed. He depicted the subterranean world in all its pomp and banality, painting the nightlife, smoky interiors, exhausted performers, and cabaret scenes. He studied the prostitutes and entertainers, their customers and clients, choosing not to focus on the gloss and the flash, but the reality behind the greasepaint. Lautrec showed the truth of life lived in the Parisian fast lane and many of the consequences of such a life.

Of his contemporaries, Lautrec most revered and admired Degas, and took from him the tilted perspective and strange physical forms with which he assembled his compositions. A particularly favorite technique of Lautrec was *peinture à l'essence,* a special mixture of oil that is diluted and thinned with turpentine. He liked to use it when working on cardboard because it emphasized his rapid brushwork and gave the painting movement and added vibrancy.

Toulouse-Lautrec's artistic output coincided with

the development of modern printmaking and the increased sophistication of advertising through lithographic posters. He was the first artist to explore and really exploit the medium. His first-known lithograph dates from 1891. He combined flat, Japanese-style images with lettering and created an entirely new and hugely influential style of poster. To make a lithograph, Lautrec made a number of preparatory sketches before preparing the complete design for the lithographer.

The design was then handed to a professional to complete the process of transferring the image onto the metal for printing. The final lithograph varied from handbill size—some personally signed by Lautrec—to poster size, and the print run could vary in number from 50 to 1,000 or more. The numbers of any given editions were not recorded and the prints were unnumbered. Lautrec did, however, put his initials, or a stamp—and occasionally his signature—on his posters.

As an adult, Lautrec's career spanned a prolific 20-year period. Among his surviving works are 737 canvases, 275 watercolors, and 363 prints and posters. In addition, his creations consists of 5,084 drawings—many of them very early artistic attempts—plus a few ceramics and a few art-glass pieces. The largest collection of his work is found in the Musée Toulouse-Lautrec in Albi.

Henri Marie Raymond de Toulouse-Lautrec-Monfa was born at home in the Chateau de Mairomé on November 24, 1864, to a wealthy aristocratic family in Albi in the Midi-Pyrénées region and the Tarn département of southwest France. His parents, Comte Alphonse de Toulouse-Lautrec and Comtesse Adèle Tapié de Celeyran, were first cousins and direct descendants of the Counts of Toulouse and Lautrec and the Viscounts of Monfa. Their consanguinity—their mothers were sisters—was almost certainly responsible for Henri's many congenital health conditions.

In 1867, the count and countess had another boy, but the baby died within the year, leaving Henri as their sole child. They eventually separated and Henri was raised by a nanny. He became somewhat wild and unruly even though he had a very privileged upbringing, surrounded by various aunts and uncles, cousins, and servants. Instead of horse riding and hunting with his father and uncles, the young Henri preferred to run around the estate and to spend time lurking in the chateau's kitchens.

Comte Alphonse was a distinctly odd man. He was remote and eccentric, prone to wearing outlandish costumes and behaving very strangely in a manner that only an aristocrat could get away with. He collected exotic weapons, hunted with falcons, and is supposed to have enjoyed washing his socks in the river, much to everyone's amusement and horror. Henri was always a weak and sickly child, and after the age of eight suffered from frequent headaches and fevers so that he was confined to bed for long periods of time. Around the same period, in 1872, Henri was sent to Paris to live with his mother, and there he started to draw and paint for the first time, discovering an aptitude for the discipline.

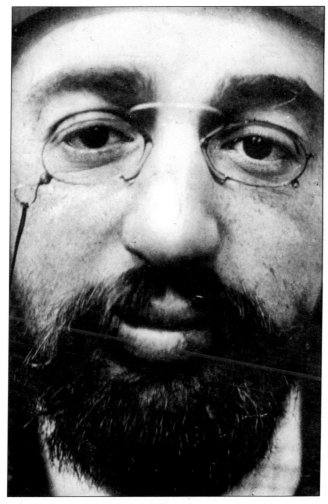

His father, grandfather, and uncle were all very capable amateur artists, and his family was initially pleased by this helpful distraction. They encouraged his talent until he expressed a desire to become a professional artist. Finally, and rather against his better judgement, his father approached René Princeteau, a family friend and professional artist, to give his son informal art lessons. Princeteau was a deaf-mute who earned his living painting sporting pictures for local society patrons. Princeteau's speciality was painting horses, and young Henri learned to love drawing them too.

Because of his delicate health it was decided that Henri and his mother should return home to Albi. Thermal baths were tried as a cure at the Roman spa town of Amélie-les-Bains in the foothills of the Pyrenees, and many doctors were consulted about how to improve Henri's health. At age 13, Henri badly fractured his left thigh bone (femur) when he fell off a chair. A year later he broke his right femur in another apparently minor accident. The consequence of these falls was that his thigh bones were unable to heal properly and his legs stopped growing, while the rest of his body grew normally. Modern scientists speculate that this was due to a rare inherited condition known as pycnodysostosis in which the bones are dense but brittle. In tribute to Lautrec, the condition has also been dubbed Toulouse-Lautrec syndrome.

Lautrec never came to terms with his short stature, and he could only walk with difficulty, using a cane. Unable to hunt and ride with his father, Henri was left free to pursue his much-preferred interests of painting and drawing. Lautrec's parents were shattered by their son's consistent and untreatable health problems; his father grew more remote, while his mother became even more attentive and devoted. In 1882, at the age of 18, encouraged by his art tutors, Henri left behind provincial Albi and moved to Paris, drawn by the city's reputation as the epicenter of artistic achievement. Highly recommended by his old tutor Rene Princeteau, Lautrec was able to take up the coveted position of student at the studio of Léon Bonnat, one of the most celebrated contemporary artists. While there, he became close friends with Louis Anquetin, who was later to become a celebrated artist. Unfortunately, Lautrec and the master soon developed a mutual dislike—so much so that, until his death in 1922, Bonnat would personally do what he could to stop Lautrec's work becoming part of any of the French national collections.

When Bonnat was made a professor at the École des Beaux-Arts, Lautrec moved—together with Anquetin—to the studio of another noted academic artist, Fernand Cormon, a much more relaxed and companionable man. He stayed for five years during which time he made the acquaintance of other would-be artists—most notably Vincent van Gogh and Émile Bernard. Cormon encouraged his students to visit art galleries and explore their surroundings for suitable subjects. As a result, Lautrec learned to paint outside—en plein air—as the Impressionists notoriously did a few years earlier. In 1884, he

took lodgings in an apartment on rue Ganneron in Montmartre—the heart of Parisian nightlife. He would remain in north Paris for the next 20 years, most of the rest of his life.

One of Lautrec's favorite painting spots was the Montmartre garden of his neighbor and retired photographer, Père Forest. Here he painted a number of portraits of the red-headed model Carmen Gaudin; she later appeared as the subject of his painting *The Laundress*. In 1887, at the end of five years with Cormon, Lautrec held an exhibition of his paintings in Toulouse, under the pseudonym "Tréclau"—an anagram of his name. The exhibition did not seem to raise any notable comment.

At first, Lautrec did not fully enter the notorious nightlife of Paris. He waited until after he graduated from Cormon's studio before plunging headlong into the decadent and sleazy side of Paris where he reveled in all its insalubrious delights. By the late 1880s, Lautrec was fully integrated into the Parisian art world and even held several exhibitions with his friends Vincent van Gogh and Louis Anquetin. From 1889 onward, he was a regular exhibitor at the Independent Artists Salon.

Lautrec soon became a familiar sight in the more risqué nightspots of Paris, smoking, drinking beer and wine, and talking to everyone, while simultaneously sketching the characters and scenes around him. He was a popular fellow, especially appreciated by his friends for his acerbic wit and self-deprecating behavior. It became his habit to sketch at night, then in his studio the following

day to work up his sketches into lithographs or paintings.

Like many contemporary Paris-based artists, Lautrec first exhibited his works on the walls of the cafés, restaurants, and bars of Montmartre. But his graphically compelling and apparently spontaneous works stood out from the other artistic offerings and quickly attracted flattering critical attention. He started to get commissions. Some of his contemporaries thought such commercial work was demeaning, but Lautrec was confident enough not to be concerned about their opinions. Money was not much of a problem for him because he enjoyed a regular income from his family, but his poster work gave him money to spare, which he happily spent on drinks and excesses of various kinds.

As time passed, Lautrec's drinking increased, so that he was soon drinking strong alcohol such as brandy and whisky and, inevitably, the dangerously seductive "green fairy," absinthe. His drinking did not stop him from drawing and painting, but it did worsen his health.

In 1887, Lautrec moved to a new studio on rue Caulaincourt, just next door to the Goupil printshop. With his growing success, Lautrec earned more money. The proceeds, when they didn't go to buying paper and paints, went to alcohol, which he was consuming in ever greater quantities. He enjoyed the nightlife and increasingly spent more time out and about at night than during the day.

In the late nineteenth century, Japanese prints became the rage in Paris. Many artists and collectors who were interested in graphics admired and bought the works of great Japanese masters of the art such as Utagawa Hiroshige and Katsushika Hokusai. Lautrec was no exception to this trend. He greatly admired the Ukiyo-e art (Japanese woodblock prints) and studied them to understand their asymmetric compositions of elegant line, startling silhouette, and flat color without shading. Lautrec was one of the first artists to incorporate these Asian styles into his own work.

Many of these Japanese prints were studies of call girls, brothels, and restaurants, as well as the theater and actors—the very same worlds that Lautrec loved and wanted to record. Lautrec took much inspiration from these prints and began using distinctly Japanese elements in his work: large flat blocks of color, strange perspectives, and elegantly minimal use of composition and line.

Lautrec benefited from the advances in the technology of lithography, such as the synthesis of new printing colors, increased subtlety in shading and effect, and the ability to print much larger posters.

The Moulin Rouge was one of the most notorious nightclubs in Montmartre. It opened in 1889 to cater to the crowds flocking into Paris to see the 1889 Exposition Universal and its iconic symbol, the Eiffel Tower. The extravagant cabaret was a huge success and attracted an international demi-monde. Lautrec was commissioned to design a series of posters to celebrate and publicize its opening. Lautrec remained the artist of choice of the Moulin

Rouge and was present most nights, wearing his characteristic bowler hat and chatting, drinking, laughing, smoking, and sketching. As the nightclub's chosen artist, he always had a reserved seat at the cabaret, and the nightclub enthusiastically exhibited his paintings around the premises. He was a popular, welcomed figure, completely accepted backstage among the dancers and singers.

Thanks in part to the Moulin Rouge posters, Lautrec became the most sought-after poster artist in Paris. He was always wanted to advertise the opening of a new burlesque or restaurant.

Lautrec knew, and was known by, everyone who mattered in Montmartre. He was friendly with many of the most interesting characters in the arrondissement. From 1890, his near-constant companion during his night-time adventures around the hotspots of the city was his tall cousin, Dr. Tapié de Celeyran. He made a portrait of his cousin—Dr. Gabriel Tapié de Celeyran—in 1894. But his preferred subjects were the women of Montmartre. An early favorite was a prostitute nicknamed La Casque d'Or (Golden Helmet), whose real name was Carmen Gaudin, whom he painted in the Montmartre garden of his friend Père Forest.

The promoters of new entertainments—and often the artists themselves—came to Lautrec to commission him for posters and billboards to paste around Paris to advertise their performances. New cafés and restaurants also commissioned him to draw posters advertising their presence.

A number of Parisian entertainers will always be associated with Lautrec. One is Yvette Gulibert, a *diseuse*, or speaker, nicknamed for her manner of semi-singing, semi-talking her way through a song. Another is Jane Avril, the great music hall performer, whom he immortalized in his poster *Divan Japonais*, with her lily-white skin, slim figure swathed in a clingy black dress, and elegant face topped by a bright red flame of hair. A third is Loïe Fuller, an American burlesque artist, who headlined at the Folies-Bergère, and was a modern dance pioneer nicknamed the Electric Fairy for her dance performances that included multicolored lights and music.

A more notorious dancer was Louise Weber (La Goulue, or "The Glutton"), who was famous for creating the outrageous Can-Can dance, and her partner the contortionist Valentin le Désossé. Lautrec painted several times the female clown and dancer Cha-U-Kao, who performed at the Moulin Rouge and the Nouveau Cirque, as well as the English singer May Belfort, whom he first met at the Café de Decadents.

Among his male subjects were his good friend and owner of Le Mirliton Café, the singer-poet Aristide Bruant, with his distinctive wide-brimmed black hat and red scarf. Typical of an era when artists and subjects tended to know and like each other, Lautrec was able to portray his subjects' gregarious and imaginative personalities.

In contrast to the glamorous stage personalities Lautrec captured on paper, but occupying much the same world, were the prostitutes of Paris, especially those of Montmartre. Lautrec depicted them in a nonjudgmental fashion, as ordinary women living a hard life. He lived in various brothels between 1892 and 1894, making sketches and paintings of the women there, showing them in all their humanity, undisguised by their professional poise. The series of brothel works entitled *Elles* dates from this period. Coming from an aristocratic background, Lautrec was a bit of an Anglophile and spoke English well enough to visit London in the 1890s. Arriving in the city as a celebrated and successful poster artist, he was immediately commissioned for a bicycle poster—*La Chaîne Simpson*—and by the stationery company J. & E. Bella to advertise their new paper confetti—instead of the previously dangerous confetti made from plaster—with the poster *Confetti*. Also during his stay in London, Lautrec met and became good friends with the intellectual wit and playwright Oscar Wilde.

His physical limitations caused Lautrec to be the frequent butt of cruel jokes. Such prejudice is often cited as one of the principal reasons for his increasingly frequent and heavy use of alcohol. His appetite for wine and beer was replaced by his love for American-style cocktails. To serve at his notorious Friday night parties, Lautrec is said to have invented the lethal Tremblement de Terre (Earthquake): three parts absinthe to three parts cognac mixed with lots of ice.

After 1897, because of his highly social nature and his increasing addiction to alcohol, Lautrec spent less time alone in his studio and more in the bars, restaurants, and dance halls. He even had a hollow cane in which to secretly carry alcohol. Thanks also to his increasingly erratic behavior, rumors started to spread that he suffered from syphilis as well as alcohol dependency.

In 1899, Toulouse-Lautrec suffered a complete nervous breakdown and was committed to a clinic in Neuilly for three months. The treatment was arranged by his mother in collusion with some of his close friends, but after his recovery he swiftly moved back to Paris. To appease his mother, and in a vain attempt to have a rest cure, Lautrec journeyed to Normandy on the Atlantic coast of France to breathe the bracing sea air, but his alcohol addiction was too ingrained. Unable to rid himself of his demons, his health only declined.

In 1901, Lautrec suffered a debilitating stroke that left him partially paralyzed. He was sent home to his mother in Albi on August 20. On September 9, with his devoted mother and a few friends at his bedside, he lay dying at the family estate at Malromé. To everyone's amazement his father appeared to say goodbye. Lautrec is reported to have remarked, "Good Papa. I knew you wouldn't miss the kill." His last remark to his father is recorded as being, "Old fool," after Count Alphonse had suggested that they cut off his beard in deference to a Muslim custom. Count Alphonse also suggested that Henri's shoelaces should be used to swat the noisy flies buzzing about the room.

Lautrec's last reported words were to his mother as he lay dying in her arms, "You mother, none other but you." Henri de Toulouse-Lautrec died from a combination of long-term alcohol abuse and syphilis at the age of 36. He was buried near his home in Verdelais, in the Gironde.

At the time of his death, Lautrec's studio in Paris still contained a huge number of his works. These became the property of his mother, the Comtesse Adèle de Celeyran. She wanted to keep the collection together and approached a number of galleries and museums to see if they wanted it: every one of them rejected the offer. Finally, in 1922, Maurice Joyant, Lautrec's art dealer, suggested to the countess that the City of Albi might take the collection. Various members of Lautrec's family also agreed to donate their paintings. The chosen site was in the thirteenth-century Palais de la Berbie, which rises above the River Tarn. The Musée Toulouse-Lautrec officially opened on July 30, 1922, and houses the largest collection (roughly 1,000 pieces) of the works of Toulouse-Lautrec.

Plate 1

ARTILLERYMAN SADDLING HIS HORSE
1879 Musee Toulouse Lautrec, Albi, France
50.5 x 37.5 cm

THE BALL
1870 Private Collection
56 x 36 cm

Plate 2

Plate 3

THE DOG (SKETCH OF TOUC)

1880 São Paulo Museum of Art, Brazil
35 x 26 cm

Plate 4

A LABORER AT CELEYRAN
1882 Musee Toulouse Lautrec, Albi, France
60 X 50 cm

Plate 5

BOUQUET OF VIOLETS IN A VASE

1882 Dallas Museum of Art
24 x 19 cm

PORTRAIT OF MADAME LA COMTESSE ADÈLE DE TOULOUSE LAUTREC Plate 6

1882 Brooklyn Museum, New York
65.4 x 43.2 cm

Plate 7

STUDY OF A NUDE
1882 Musee Toulouse Lautrec, Albi, France
55 x 46 cm

Plate 8

YOUNG ROUTY
1882 Neue Pinakothek, Munich
61 x 49.8 cm

Plate 9

GUSTAVE LUCIEN DENNERY

1883 Musée d'Orsay, Paris

Plate 10

JARDIN DE PARIS, MAY BELFORT, PLAKAT
1883 Yale University Art Gallery
130 x 95 cm

Plate 11

THE BIG MARIA, VENUS MINTMARTRE

1884, Von Der Heydt Museum, Wuppertal, Germany

80.7 x 64.8 cm

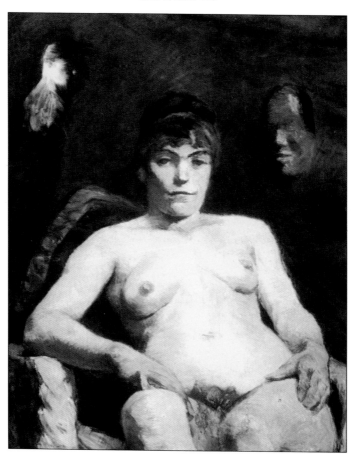

Plate 12

BALLET DANCERS
1885 Art Institute of Chicago
153.5 x 152.5 cm

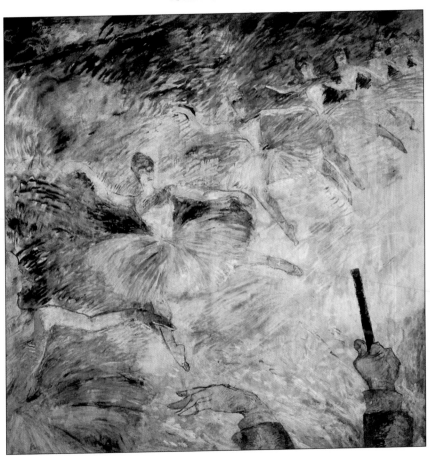

Plate 13

EMILE BERNARD
1885 The Tate, London
54.4 x 43.5 cm

PORTRAIT OF JEANNE WENZ
188 Art Institute of Chicago
80.7 x 59.5 cm

Plate 14

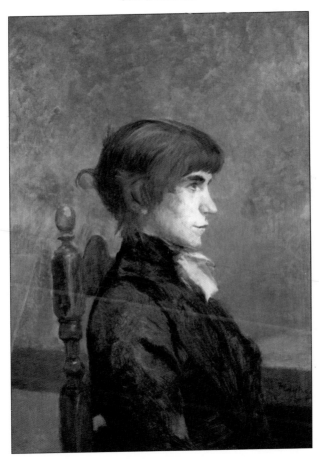

Plate 15

PORTRAIT OF VINCENT VAN GOGH

1887 Van Gogh Museum, Amsterdam
54 x 45 cm

AT THE CIRQUE FERNANDO, RIDER ON A WHITE HORSE

Plate 16

1888 Norton Simon Museum, Pasadena, CA

60 x 79.5 cm

Plate 17

THE REDHEAD WITH A WHITE BLOUSE

1888 Museum of Fine Arts, Boston
55.9 x 46.7 cm

Plate 18

AT LA BASTILLE (PORTRAIT OF JEANNE WENZ)

1889 National Gallery of Art, Washington DC
72.5 x 49.5 cm

Plate 19

BALL AT THE MOULIN DE LA GALETTE
1889 Art Institute of Chicago
88.9 x 101.3 cm

Plate 20

THE HANGOVER (SUZANNE VALADON)

1889 Harvard Art Museum/Fogg Museum, Cambridge, MA
45.1 x 53.3 cm

Plate 21

THE ACTOR HENRY SAMARY

1889 Musée d'Orsay, Paris
75 x 52 cm

AT THE MOULIN ROUGE, THE DANCE
1890 Philadelphia Museum of Art
115.5 x 150 cm

Plate 22

Plate 23

SEATED WOMAN IN THE GARDEN OF MR. FOREST JUSTINE DIEUHL

1890 Musée d'Orsay, Paris
74 x 58 cm

Plate 24

AT THE NOUVEAU CIRQUE, THE DANCER AND FIVE STUFFED SHIRTS

1891 Philadelphia Museum of Art
60 x 40 cm

Plate 25

THE LAST CRUMBS

1891 Museum of Fine Arts, Boston
53.5 x 68 cm

THE STREETWALKER (ALSO KNOWN AS CASQUE D'OR) Plate 26
1890 Metropolitan Museum of Art
64.8 x 53.3 cm

Plate 27

WOMAN IN THE GARDEN
1891 National Gallery of Art, Washington DC
66 x 52.5 cm

Plate 28

WOMAN WITH GLOVES (HONORINE PLATZER)

1891 Musée d'Orsay, Paris
54 x 40 cm

Plate 29

AMBASSADEURS ARISTIDE BRUANT IN HIS CABARET
1892

CORNER IN THE MOULIN DE LA GALETTE

Plate 30

1892 National Gallery of Art, Washington DC
100 x 89.2 cm

Plate 31

IN BED
1893 Musée d'Orsay, Paris
54 x 70.5 cm

JANE AVRIL DANCING
1892 Musee du Louvre
85.5 x 45 cm

Plate 32

Plate 33

JANE AVRIL ENTERS THE MOULIN ROUGE

1892 The Courtauld Gallery, London
102 x 55 cm

LA GOULUE ARRIVING AT THE MOULIN ROUGE WITH TWO WOMEN Plate 34

1892 Museum of Modern Art, New York
79.4 x 59.0 cm

WOMAN WITH A BLACK BOA

1892 Musée d'Orsay, Paris
60.96 x 91.44 cm

Plate 36

Plate 37

CADIEUX
1893 San Diego Museum of Art

Plate 38

MONSIEUR BOILEAU
1893 Cleveland Museum of Art
80 x 65 cm

Plate 39

ALFRED LA GUIGNE

1894 National Gallery of Art, Washington DC
64.5 x 49.5 cm

Plate 40

BABYLON GERMAN BY VICTOR JOZE

1894 Brooklyn Museum, New York
124.5 x 87.6 cm

Plate 41

LA GOULUE AND PAUL LESCAU

1894 National Museum of Fine Arts, Buenos Aires
55 x 43.5 cm

Plate 42

PROSTITUTES AROUND A DINNER TABLE

1882 Museum of Fine Arts, Budapest
60.3 x 80 cm

Plate 43

YVETTE GUIBERT SINGING

1894 Pushkin Museum of Fine Art, Moscow
57 x 42 cm

Plate 44

DANCE AT THE MOULIN ROUGE
1895 Musée d'Orsay, Paris
298 x 316 cm

Plate 45

MARCELLE LENDER
1895 Yale University Art Gallery
32.5 x 24 cm

Plate 46

THE CLOWNESSE CHA U KAO AT THE MOULIN ROUGE

1895 Musée d'Orsay, Paris
64 x 49 cm

Plate 47

THE PROMENOIR THE MOULIN ROUGE

1895 Art Institute of Chicago
123 x 140.5 cm

TWO FRIENDS
1895 E.G. Buhrle Collection, Zurich
64.5 x 84 cm

Plate 48

Plate 49

ALONE (ELLES)

1896 Musée d'Orsay, Paris
31 X 39.6 cm

MAXIME DETHOMAS AT THE BALL OF THE OPERA

Plate 50

1896 National Gallery of Art, Washington DC
67.5 x 62.5 cm

Plate 51

NAPOLÉON
1896 E.G. Buhrle Collection, Zurich
59.3 x 46 cm

PORTRAIT OF CIPA GODEBSKY
1896 Cleveland Museum of Art
57 x 45 cm

Plate 52

Plate 53

THE SOFA

1896 Metropolitan Museum of Art
62.9 x 81 cm

THE WOMAN LOOKING INTO A HAND-HELD MIRROR Plate 54

1896 Brooklyn Museum, New York
52.2 x 40 cm

Plate 55

THE WOMAN WITH A TUB

1896 Brooklyn Museum, New York
39.8 x 52.1 cm

Plate 56

WOMAN AT HER TOILET

1896 Musée d'Orsay, Paris
67 x 54 cm

Plate 57

CROUCHING WOMAN WITH RED HAIR

1897 San Diego Museum of Art
47 x 60 cm

Plate 58

MADEMOISELLE BEATRICE TAPIE DE CELEYRAN

1897 Private Collection
23.81 x 16.51 cm

Plate 59

PAUL LECLERCQ
1897 Musée d'Orsay, Paris
54 X 67 cm

PORTRAIT OF BERTHE BADY
1897 Musee Toulouse Lautrec, Albi, France
69 x 58 cm

Plate 60

Plate 61

RECLINING NUDE
1897 The Barnes Foundation, Merion, PA

Plate 62

AT THE CAFE, THE CUSTOMER AND THE ANEMIC CASHIER

1898 Kunsthaus, Zurich
81.5 x 60 cm

Plate 63
DINNER AT THE HOUSE OF M. AND MME. NATHANSON

1898 Museum of Fine Arts, Houston
60 x 80 cm

MADAME POUPOULE AT HER DRESSING TABLE

Plate 64

1898 Musee Toulouse Lautrec, Albi, France
60.8 x 49.6 cm

Plate 65 THE SINGING LESSON: THE TEACHER, MLLE.DIHAU, WITH MME.FAVERAUD

1898 Mohammed Mahmoud Khalil Museum, Cairo
75.7 x 69 cm

Plate 66

AMAZONE
1899 The Tate, London
55.5 x 42.5 cm

Plate 67

AT THE RACES

1899 Musee Toulouse Lautrec, Albi, France
34 X 44 cm

Plate 68

TETE-A-TETE SUPPER
1899 Courtauld Institute of Art, London
73.5 X 46 cm

Plate 69

ROMAIN COOLUS

1899 Musee Toulouse Lautrec, Albi, France

55 x 35 cm

Plate 70

THE JOCKEY
1899 Brooklyn Museum, New York
51.5 x 36 cm

Plate 71

THE MEDICAL INSPECTION (RUE DES MOULINS)

1894 National Gallery of Art, Washington DC

83.5 x 61.4 cm

Plate 72

THE PRAYER

1894 Musee Toulouse Lautrec, Albi, France
111.5 × 132.5 cm

Plate 73

MESSALINE
1901 E.G. Buhrle Collection, Zurich

Plate 74

OBSERVATION M.FABRE, RESERVE OFFICER

1901 National Museum of Fine Arts, Buenos Aires
60.5 x 49.5 cm

Plate 75

PORTRAIT OF OCTAVE RAQUIN

1901 São Paulo Museum of Art, Brazil
34 X 44 cm

Plate 76

MISS EGLANTINE TROUPE
Yale University Art Gallery

Plate 77
AN EXAMINATION AT THE FACULTY OF MEDICINE, PARIS
1901 Musee Toulouse Lautrec, Albi, France
65 x 81 cm

Plate 78

THE MILLINER

1900 Musee Toulouse Lautrec, Albi, France
60 X 50 cm

Plate 79

MAURICE JOYANT SOMME BAY
1900 Musee Toulouse Lautrec, Albi, France
116.5 x 81 cm

Plate 80

THE LADY OF THE STAR HARBOUR

1899 Musee Toulouse Lautrec, Albi, France

41 x 32.8 cm

Plate 81

AT THE CIRCUS, HORSE AND MONKEY DRESSAGE

1899
35.5 x 25 cm

Plate 82

ADMIRAL VIAUD
1901 São Paulo Museum of Art, Brazil

INDEX